Men, Women and Children
in
Tudor
Times

Jane Bingham

WAYLAND

KT-362-249

First published in 2010 by Wayland
Copyright © Wayland 2010

This paperback edition published in
2011 by Wayland

Wayland
338 Euston Road
London NW1 3BH

Wayland
Level 17/207 Kent Street
Sydney, NSW 2000

All rights reserved

British Library Cataloguing in Publication Data
Bingham, Jane
   Men, women and children in the Tudor times.
   1. Great Britain - History - Tudors, 1485-1603- Juvenile literature
   2. Great Britain - Social conditions - 16th century - Juvenile literature
   3. Great Britain - Social life and customs - 16th century - Juvenile literature.
   I. Title
   942'.05-dc22
   ISBN: 978 0 7502 6707 6

Printed in China

Wayland is a division of Hachette Children's Books, an Hachette UK Company.
www.hachette.co.uk

The Art Archive/Marquess of Bath/Eileen Tweedy: 8; The Art Archive/Musée de Chateau de Versailles/Gianni dagli
Orti: 23; The Art Gallery Collection/Alamy: Cover (Main), title page, 6, 10, 27; John Bethell/Bridgeman Art Library,
London: 12; Ian M. Butterfield/Alamy: 26; The Crown Estate/Bridgeman Art Library, London: 21; The Granger
Collection/TopFoto/TopFoto.co.uk: Cover (TL), 15, 17, 18; Robert Harding World Imagery/Corbis: 16; Hardwick Hall,
Derbyshire, UK/National Trust/Bridgeman Art Library, London: 13; The National Trust Photolibrary/John Bethell/Alamy:
9; North Wind Picture Archives/Alamy: Cover (B), 20; PCL/Alamy: 25; The Print Collector/Alamy: Cover (BL), 19, 22
Private Collection, © Look & Learn/Bridgeman Art Library, London: 14 ©2003 Topham Picturepoint/TopFoto.co.uk: 24;
The Trustees of Weston Park Foundation, UK/Bridgeman Art Library, London: 11; Yale Center for British Art, Paul
Mellon Collection, USA/Bridgeman Art Library, London: 7

CONTENTS

WHO WERE THE TUDORS?   6

TUDOR MEN, WOMEN AND CHILDREN?   8

WHO WAS IN CHARGE IN TUDOR TIMES?   10

WHAT WAS LIFE LIKE IN A TUDOR FAMILY?   12

DID TUDOR CHILDREN GO TO SCHOOL?   16

WHAT JOBS DID TUDOR PEOPLE DO?   18

WHAT DID TUDOR ADULTS AND CHILDREN WEAR?   22

HOW DID TUDOR ADULTS AND CHILDREN HAVE FUN?   24

HOW IMPORTANT WAS RELIGION FOR THE TUDORS?   26

GLOSSARY   28

FURTHER INFORMATION AND
PLACES TO VISIT   29

INDEX   30

Words that appear in **bold**
can be found in the glossary
on page 28.

WHO WERE THE TUDORS?

The Tudors were a family of kings and queens who ruled England between 1485 and 1603. This important time in English history is known as the Tudor period. Nowadays, the term "the Tudors" also has a wider meaning. It covers all the men, women and children who lived in Tudor times.

▲ This Tudor painting shows people at a wedding feast. The wealthy guests are being waited on by servants.

TUDOR TIMES

During the Tudor period, towns and trade grew dramatically. Tudor monarchs encouraged drama, poetry and music, and adventurous sailors reached new lands. There were also some major changes in the English Church.

RICH AND POOR

Wealthy Tudor families lived in comfort in large houses, wore fashionable clothes, and ate good food. Their children were well educated. Life was very different for the poor. Children from poor families started work very young. Many people went hungry and died from disease.

THE TUDOR TIMELINE

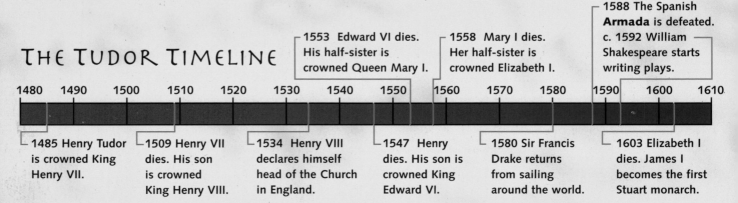

1553 Edward VI dies. His half-sister is crowned Queen Mary I.

1558 Mary I dies. Her half-sister is crowned Elizabeth I.

1588 The Spanish **Armada** is defeated.
c. 1592 William Shakespeare starts writing plays.

| 1480 | 1490 | 1500 | 1510 | 1520 | 1530 | 1540 | 1550 | 1560 | 1570 | 1580 | 1590 | 1600 | 1610 |

1485 Henry Tudor is crowned King Henry VII.

1509 Henry VII dies. His son is crowned King Henry VIII.

1534 Henry VIII declares himself head of the Church in England.

1547 Henry dies. His son is crowned King Edward VI.

1580 Sir Francis Drake returns from sailing around the world.

1603 Elizabeth I dies. James I becomes the first Stuart monarch.

TUDOR KINGS AND QUEENS

Altogether, there were five Tudor **monarchs**. Henry VII became King of England following a violent struggle for power. After Henry's death, his son, Henry VIII, reigned for the next 38 years. Then Henry VIII's three children each ruled in turn. First his son Edward became king, but he died very young. Edward VI was followed by Mary I and then by Elizabeth I. Elizabeth I had no children to **inherit** the throne. When she died, in 1603, the rule of the Tudors ended.

▲ This painting shows King Henry VIII and his three children. The painting is not meant to be a realistic family portrait. Instead, Mary, Edward and Elizabeth are shown as they looked when they ruled England.

REAL LIVES

EDWARD VI: A BOY KING

Edward VI was the son of King Henry VIII and his third wife, Jane Seymour. His mother died very soon after he was born, so he was brought up by **ladies-in-waiting**. From the age of six, Edward had lessons from private **tutors**. He was a clever and hard-working boy. When Edward was nine, his father died. The child was crowned king, but his powerful guardians kept strict control over him. In January 1553, he developed tuberculosis (a serious lung disease) and died six months later, aged 15.

TUDOR MEN, WOMEN AND CHILDREN

Family life was at the heart of Tudor society, and people of all classes lived in large families. Tudor men, women and children all knew their place within their family group.

◀ This portrait shows a wealthy Tudor nobleman with his family. Even the family pets have been included in the portrait!

TUDOR MEN

Tudor men were recognized as the head of the household. A Tudor man expected his wife and children to obey him totally. Even uncles and older brothers could expect instant obedience from the girls in the family. In return for their position of respect, men were expected to provide enough money for their family to live on.

TUDOR WOMEN

Most Tudor women stayed at home and ran their household. If they were wealthy, they relied on their servants to do most of the work. Poorer women did all the housework, **laundry** and cooking themselves, with their daughters' help. Some wives from poorer families also helped their husbands in their daily work.

TUDOR CHILDREN

Tudor boys and girls were expected to be quiet and obedient. In poor families, they also had to be useful. Sons and daughters as young as five years old were given jobs to do. Children of all classes had very little freedom in their lives. Usually, a boy's parents chose what kind of work he would do. Parents also decided who their children should marry – especially if the children came from a wealthy family. Girls often married around the age of 14. Boys usually waited longer, marrying when they were in their twenties.

REAL LIVES

BESS OF HARDWICK: A NOBLEWOMAN

Bess of Hardwick was the third surviving daughter of the owner of Hardwick Hall, in Derbyshire. When she was 12 years old, Bess married the 14-year-old Robert Barlow, a sickly boy who died four years later, leaving her a fortune. Bess went on to marry three more times, and each new husband was richer than the last. She ended up marrying the Earl of Shrewsbury. Altogether, Bess had eight children, but two of them died as babies.

WHO WAS IN CHARGE IN TUDOR TIMES?

The most important person in Tudor society was the monarch. The Tudor king or queen was surrounded by the royal **court**, a group of advisors drawn from the grandest families in England. The other powerful people in Tudor society were cardinals and archbishops, leaders of the English Church.

THE MONARCH DECIDES

The Tudor kings and queens took important decisions about the way England was run. All laws had to be approved by the monarch. The king or queen decided how their people should worship and whether their country should go to war.

ADVISORS AT THE COURT

All the Tudor monarchs relied heavily on their advisors. These advisors were clever men who helped the monarch to make good decisions and kept a look out for enemies.

▼ This painting shows King Henry VIII surrounded by his courtiers as he arrives for a meeting with the King of France.

King Henry VIII had three main advisors: Thomas Wolsey, Thomas Cromwell and Sir Thomas Moore. These men had great power, but advising the king was a risky business. Henry quarrelled bitterly with Cromwell and Moore and gave orders for them to be beheaded.

CHURCH LEADERS

In Tudor times, the Church was very important in everybody's life. So the Church leaders had great power. Thomas Wolsey was a cardinal in the **Roman Catholic Church**, but Henry VIII also made him his **chancellor**, putting him in charge of the royal fortunes.

▲ Cromwell was unusual because he was born poor, but managed to rise to a position of great power. Most royal advisors in the Tudor period came from noble families.

REAL LIVES

THOMAS CROMWELL: ROYAL ADVISOR

Thomas Cromwell came from a poor family. He worked abroad as a soldier and a merchant, before returning to London to study law. When he was about 30 years old, he became legal secretary to Cardinal Wolsey. Cromwell worked at gaining the king's confidence and in 1532 he was made King Henry VIII's chief minister. As Henry's main advisor, Cromwell urged the king to make himself head of the English Church (see page 26). Then, in 1540, Cromwell persuaded Henry to marry Anne of Cleves, but the marriage was a disaster. Henry turned against Cromwell and gave orders for him to be executed.

WHAT WAS LIFE LIKE IN A TUDOR FAMILY?

Families in Tudor times were generally large. It was not unusual for a couple to have ten or more babies, but it was rare for all their children to survive. In many families, grandparents and unmarried uncles and aunts also shared the family home.

FAMILY HOMES

▲ Grand Tudor houses were often built from brick, with large windows and tall chimneys. Poorer homes were built from plaster and beams.

Tudor family homes ranged from enormous mansions, to tiny, tumbledown shacks. Wealthy families had lots of fine furniture, including solid tables and chairs, chests for storing clothes, and four-poster beds. Poor families had almost no furniture. Sometimes the whole family shared the same bed.

The country homes of the rich were set in beautiful grounds. They had gardens for flowers and herbs, and even – in some cases – a hunting park. Poor people's cottages had small gardens where they kept chickens and grew vegetables.

BABIES AND TODDLERS

The first few years of a child's life were filled with danger, as babies often died from colds and diseases. Newborn babies slept in wooden cradles and wore swaddling clothes – tightly wound strips of cotton that kept their arms close to their sides. Babies in wealthy families had silver rattles and teething rings. Toddlers had wooden walkers with wheels to help them move around.

BOYS AND GIRLS

Boys and girls found lots of ways to have fun – even when their parents had very little money. They played with rag dolls and swords made from wood. They blew up pig bladders to make footballs, and they used pebbles to play games of jacks. Skittles and hopscotch were other popular games, and wealthy children had sets of playing cards and chess.

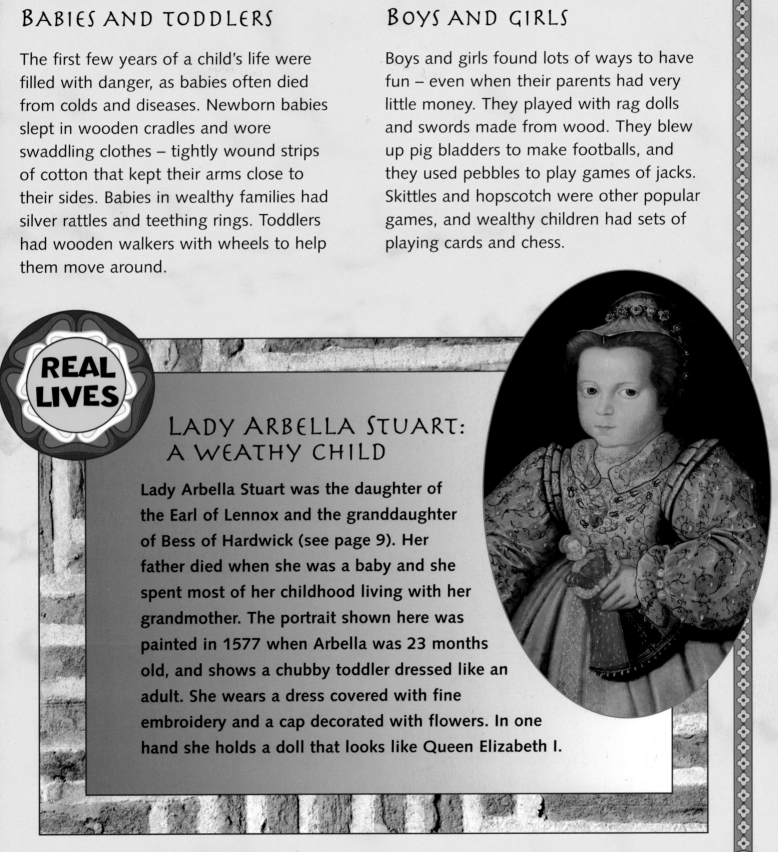

REAL LIVES

LADY ARBELLA STUART: A WEATHY CHILD

Lady Arbella Stuart was the daughter of the Earl of Lennox and the granddaughter of Bess of Hardwick (see page 9). Her father died when she was a baby and she spent most of her childhood living with her grandmother. The portrait shown here was painted in 1577 when Arbella was 23 months old, and shows a chubby toddler dressed like an adult. She wears a dress covered with fine embroidery and a cap decorated with flowers. In one hand she holds a doll that looks like Queen Elizabeth I.

HARD CHILDHOODS

Life was very tough for the children of the poor. Without good food or proper clothes and shoes, they suffered terribly from cold in the winter. Many of their homes were breeding grounds for germs – especially in the cities. People threw their waste into the city streets, and rats and flies spread diseases.

FAMILY SERVANTS

Wealthy people relied on large numbers of servants to run their homes. Maids cleaned the house and did the laundry. Ladies' maids dressed the mistress of the house and menservants looked after the master. **Gamekeepers** provided a steady supply of birds and animals for the family to eat.

▲ This painting by a modern artist shows Queen Mary I in a London street. The contrast between rich and poor is strong.

FOOD FOR THE RICH

Cooks prepared and cooked the meals for wealthy families. For breakfast and supper, rich people usually ate bread, beef and beer. Dinner was served soon after 11 o'clock and was the main meal of the day. It included a lot of meat, which had been preserved by salting, smoking or drying.

Vegetables were not popular with the rich, as they thought of them as poor people's food. When a noble family entertained guests, their cooks prepared a feast of up to 30 different dishes, mainly made from meat and fish.

FOOD FOR THE POOR

Poor families did not have a varied diet. They ate bread or porridge for most meals, washed down with water or beer. Country families enjoyed a better diet, because they could eat their own eggs and vegetables, as well as small amounts of meat, such as rabbit or crow.

▲ In Tudor times, people often died young. This family portrait shows a husband with his second wife, but also includes his dead first wife lying on her bed.

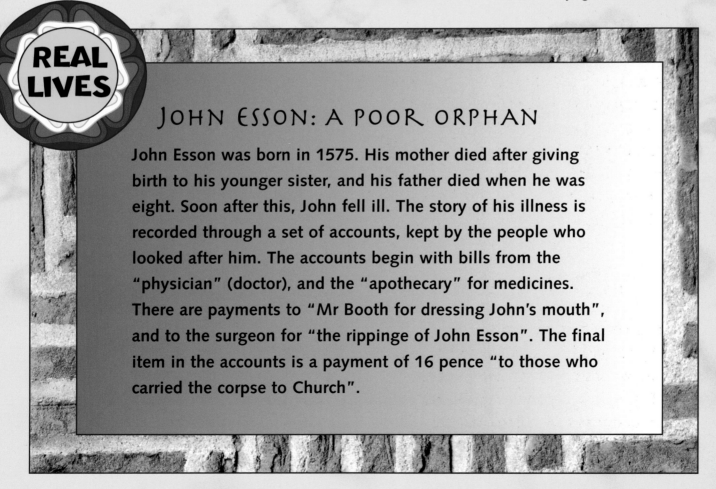

REAL LIVES

JOHN ESSON: A POOR ORPHAN

John Esson was born in 1575. His mother died after giving birth to his younger sister, and his father died when he was eight. Soon after this, John fell ill. The story of his illness is recorded through a set of accounts, kept by the people who looked after him. The accounts begin with bills from the "physician" (doctor), and the "apothecary" for medicines. There are payments to "Mr Booth for dressing John's mouth", and to the surgeon for "the rippinge of John Esson". The final item in the accounts is a payment of 16 pence "to those who carried the corpse to Church".

Did Tudor children go to school?

There were no free schools in Tudor times, so only the rich could afford to educate their children. Boys and girls from noble families were taught at home by private tutors. Merchants and lawyers paid for their sons to go to school, but there were no schools for girls.

▲ This schoolroom still looks the same as it did in Tudor times. Pupils sat at benches and learnt their lessons by heart.

Lessons at home

The best tutors of all were hired to teach the royal children. Princess Elizabeth was taught by leading **scholars** from Cambridge University. She had lessons in French, Spanish, Latin and Greek, history, arithmetic, music and theology (religious studies). Elizabeth was not always taught alone. Sometimes she shared her lessons with her brother Edward and the sons of the Duke of Northumberland.

Petty schools

At the age of five, boys from fairly well-off families were sent to 'petty school', where they learnt to read and write. These small local schools were usually run by the village priest and took pupils up to the age of seven. From there, some boys went on to study at a 'grammar school'.

GRAMMAR SCHOOLS

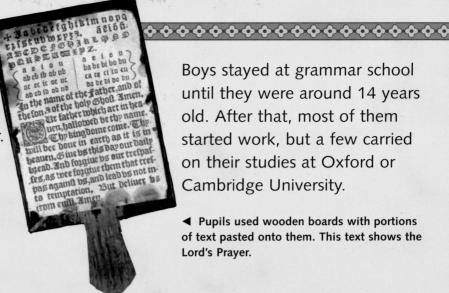

Pupils at grammar school spent a lot of time studying Latin grammar. Latin was the language used by lawyers, so it was very important to understand it. They also practised arithmetic and rhetoric (the art of public speaking).

Boys stayed at grammar school until they were around 14 years old. After that, most of them started work, but a few carried on their studies at Oxford or Cambridge University.

◀ Pupils used wooden boards with portions of text pasted onto them. This text shows the Lord's Prayer.

REAL LIVES

JOHN SKELTON: TEACHER, SCHOLAR AND POET

John Skelton studied at both Oxford and Cambridge Universities. He was an outstanding scholar and when he was about 28 years old, he was made tutor to Prince Henry (who would later become Henry VIII). Skelton taught Henry for five years and wrote several books about the art of teaching. In 1509 King Henry made him 'Orator regius' – an early version of today's Poet Laureate. Skelton wrote many poems for national occasions, but his greatest talent was for comic verse. He spent his last years as a country priest.

What Jobs did Tudor People do?

Most people in Tudor times worked on the land, but during the 16th century many people moved to the towns in search of new work. Tudor towns were full of shops and workshops, and lawyers, clerks and doctors lived and worked in town. Even beggars and thieves found that crowded city streets were good places to make a living.

▲ Many people lived in small country cottages and raised cows, goats and sheep.

Working on the Land

For poor people living in the country, life was very hard. Most of them worked as poorly paid labourers for their local landowner. Men, women and children spent long, back-breaking hours in the fields, or rose early to look after animals.

Clerks and Lawyers

As the towns grew, there was plenty of work for clerks and lawyers. Clerks worked for the king and his **ministers**, making sure that the country ran smoothly. Lawyers settled arguments between business partners and families. Most written documents were in Latin, so lawyers and clerks had to have a good education.

DOCTORS AND APOTHECARIES

Doctors in Tudor times did not really understand why people fell ill. They believed that diseases were caused by 'bad blood' and they treated their patients by bleeding them (draining large amounts of blood from their body). Some doctors used saws and knives to perform operations, but they had no **antiseptics**, so patients often died from **infection**.

▲ This picture shows a busy apothecary's shop. While the apothecary talks to his customers his assistants grind up herbs and prepare medicines.

Apothecaries were early pharmacists. They created ointments and medicines from a range of herbs and minerals. Some of their medicines worked well. Others, such as ointments made with **mercury**, made people very ill.

REAL LIVES

THOMAS ALSOP: APOTHECARY

Thomas Alsop had an apothecary's shop in London. By 1538 he was supplying medicine for Prince Edward (later Edward VI). Two years later he became King Henry VIII's apothecary, and was paid an annual fee of £26. Alsop kept detailed records of the medicines he supplied to the king. For example, almond oil to rub on Henry's lips, rhubarb pills to ease **constipation**, and soothing herbs for the king's baths. Alsop also supplied sugar candy as a treat for the royal hunting hounds.

SHOPKEEPERS AND CRAFTWORKERS

Butchers, bakers, fishmongers and brewers set up permanent shops in town, while fruit, milk and cheese were usually sold on market stalls. Keeping a shop was a family activity, with all the family members lending a hand.

Craftworkers of all kinds established workshops. Carpenters, potters and tinsmiths made furniture, pots and pans. Leatherworkers made shoes, belts and bags, and tailors sewed cloth into clothes. At the more expensive end of the market, skilled metalworkers made delicate jewellery, and fine swords and armour.

▲ This city scene shows a tailor, a barber and a furrier (fur-maker) at work. The families of craftworkers and shopkeepers usually lived in rooms above the shop.

MERCHANTS AND SEA CAPTAINS

During the Tudor period, foreign trade grew very fast. Merchants travelled all over the known world, bringing back luxury goods, such as spices, silk and silver.

Daring sea captains sailed in search of new lands, where merchants could trade. They also acted as pirates, seizing the **cargo** of other country's trading ships. Several English captains reached North and South America. They brought back potatoes, tomatoes, sweetcorn, chillies and tobacco.

SOLDIERS AND SAILORS

Tudor soldiers had to train very hard. They used canons and longbows to shoot at their enemies from a distance. For hand-to-hand fighting, they used swords, daggers and long spears called pikes.

Sailors in the royal navy lived in crowded, dirty cabins. They had to fire heavy canons at enemy ships. Small boys worked as "powder monkeys", running very fast between the ship's decks to hand out gunpowder during a battle.

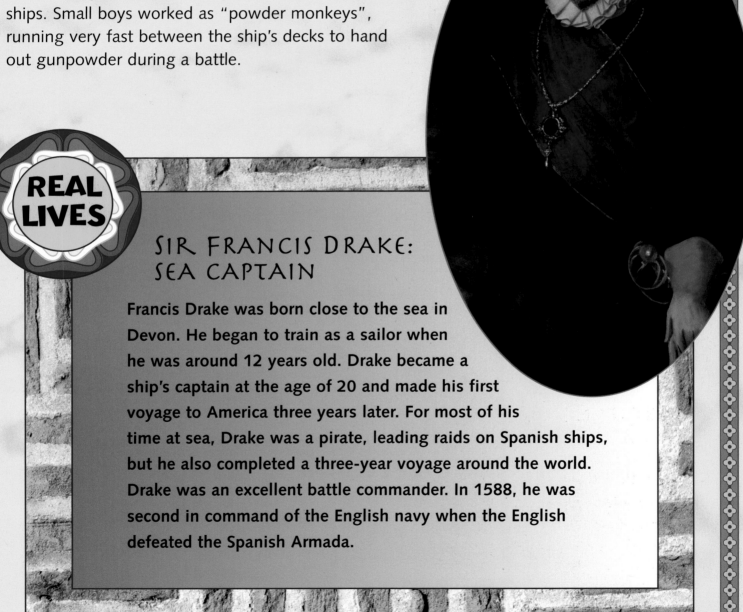

▼ Sir Francis Drake was an outstanding sea captain. In 1580, Queen Elizabeth I made him a knight after he sailed all the way round the world.

REAL LIVES

SIR FRANCIS DRAKE: SEA CAPTAIN

Francis Drake was born close to the sea in Devon. He began to train as a sailor when he was around 12 years old. Drake became a ship's captain at the age of 20 and made his first voyage to America three years later. For most of his time at sea, Drake was a pirate, leading raids on Spanish ships, but he also completed a three-year voyage around the world. Drake was an excellent battle commander. In 1588, he was second in command of the English navy when the English defeated the Spanish Armada.

WHAT DID TUDOR ADULTS AND CHILDREN WEAR?

Wealthy men and women in Tudor times wore fashionable clothes, made from the finest fabrics. Poor people had ragged clothes, usually made from rough woollen cloth. Children of all classes wore smaller versions of their parents' clothes.

▲ This image of a nobleman giving money to a beggar shows the difference between the clothes of the very rich and the very poor.

WORKING CLOTHES

Strict clothing laws banned working people from wearing colourful clothes made from fine fabrics. The law stated that workers' clothes must be made from the cheapest materials and had to be coloured with natural dyes. So poor people's clothes were made from wool, sheepskin and linen and were brown, yellow, orange, green or bluey-grey.

Poor men and boys wore simple tunics and tights. Women and girls wore long, woollen dresses, often with an apron and a cloth bonnet.

FASHIONS AT COURT

The Tudor royal court was a showcase for all the latest fashions. Both men and women wore starched cotton ruffs. Men wore a loose white shirt, a tight-fitting jacket (called a doublet), padded trousers (called breeches) and tights (called hose).

Women wore a petticoat, a bodice (or blouse) and a long skirt, supported by wooden hoops so that it stuck out a long way from the body. Over these went a floor-length gown. Fashionable clothes for men and women were made from silk, cotton and velvet and were richly decorated with jewels and embroidery.

TUDOR JEWELLERY

Tudor clothing laws only allowed the royal family and the nobility to wear jewellery in public. Noblewomen wore necklaces, brooches, earrings and rings. Noblemen wore rings and pendants, and sometimes a single pearl earring.

▼ Queen Elizabeth I was famous for her amazing clothes. This dress, decorated with eyes and ears, gave people the message that the queen could see and hear everything that happened in her kingdom.

REAL LIVES

QUEEN ELIZABETH I

Elizabeth was crowned queen when she was 25 years old, and ruled until her death, aged 69. She always made sure that she looked magnificent, but as she grew older, this effect became much harder to achieve. In the final years of her life, Queen Elizabeth wore a wig, covered her face with a thick, white paste, and painted her cheeks and lips bright red. Unfortunately, the paste she wore on her face was made from lead, which slowly poisoned her.

How did Tudor adults and children have fun?

Most people in Tudor times found time to have fun. Even poor families took time off from work to visit a travelling fair. Noblemen enjoyed hunting with friends. They also held lavish feasts with musicians and jesters to entertain their guests.

Sports and games

Poor men and boys practised archery and wrestling, and played wild games of hockey and football. Men of noble birth enjoyed fencing and tennis. King Henry VIII was so passionate about tennis that he had his own court built in his royal palace.

▼ This painting shows two young Tudor men playing tennis on a special court surrounded by high walls.

Public entertainments

Jousting tournaments were a favourite entertainment of the Tudor nobles. In these mock battles, men on horseback dressed up in armour and charged at each other. Poorer people watched displays of bear-baiting and cock-fighting. In Tudor times, people were not shocked by shows involving cruelty to animals.

MUSIC AND DRAMA

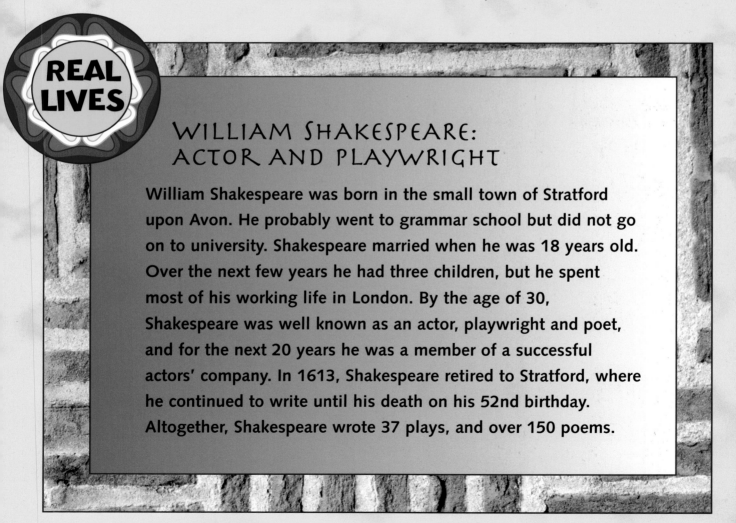

▲ The Globe Theatre in London was recently been rebuilt so that it looks just like it did in Shakespeare's time.

People of all classes loved to make music. Wealthy boys and girls learned to play an instrument, such as the lute, the recorder or the virginals (an early keyboard instrument). Poorer people often played the bagpipes.

The reign of Queen Elizabeth I was a great time for drama, and people flocked to the theatre to see the latest plays. There were several outstanding playwrights in the Tudor period, but the greatest of them all was William Shakespeare.

REAL LIVES

WILLIAM SHAKESPEARE: ACTOR AND PLAYWRIGHT

William Shakespeare was born in the small town of Stratford upon Avon. He probably went to grammar school but did not go on to university. Shakespeare married when he was 18 years old. Over the next few years he had three children, but he spent most of his working life in London. By the age of 30, Shakespeare was well known as an actor, playwright and poet, and for the next 20 years he was a member of a successful actors' company. In 1613, Shakespeare retired to Stratford, where he continued to write until his death on his 52nd birthday. Altogether, Shakespeare wrote 37 plays, and over 150 poems.

How important was religion for the Tudors?

Religion played a very important part in the lives of Tudor men, women and children. In the 16th century, some dramatic changes took place in the English Church, which split the country into two different groups. People of all classes quarrelled bitterly about religion and some men and women were even put to death because of their beliefs.

An independent church

At the start of the Tudor period, people in England belonged to the Roman Catholic Church, with the Pope at its head. But this changed when the Pope refused to allow King Henry VIII to divorce his wife. In 1534, Henry broke away from the Roman Catholic Church and founded the Church of England with himself as its head.

Conflict in England

Henry's dramatic move caused great confusion. Some people wanted to stay loyal to the Catholic Church. Others were happy to recognize Henry as the head of the Church. Members of Henry's Church of England became known as **Protestants**. Throughout the rest of the Tudor period, there was terrible conflict between Catholics and Protestants.

▲ The Tudor Protestants read the Bible in English, but Catholics were expected to read it in Latin. William Tyndale, shown here, was a leading Protestant who translated the Bible into English.

RELIGIOUS HATRED

When Queen Mary came to the throne in 1553, she made England a Roman Catholic country again. Protestants were punished for their faith, and around 280 people were executed, mainly by burning. This persecution continued until Mary's death, in 1558. She was followed by Elizabeth I, who made England a Protestant country again. Elizabeth did not persecute Roman Catholics. But some English Catholics hated having a Protestant ruler, and plotted to overthrow the queen.

▶ Queen Mary was sometimes known as 'Bloody Mary' because of all the Protestants she put to death.

REAL LIVES

JOAN WASTE: A BRAVE PROTESTANT

Joan was the daughter of a ropemaker in Derby. She was born blind but by the age of twelve she had learnt to make ropes. She attended a Protestant church, but when Queen Mary came to the throne, her local church became Roman Catholic. This meant all its services were held in Latin, and Joan complained. Joan also owned a copy of the Bible in English, which she paid her friends to read to her, and this was forbidden by the Catholic Church. Joan was sentenced to death for her Protestant beliefs. She walked bravely to her death, holding her twin brother's hand.

Glossary

antiseptic: an ointment that fights germs

archbishops: the most important priests in the Church of England

armada: a large group of sailing ships. The Spanish Armada set sail as part of an unsuccessful attempt by Philip II of Spain to invade England in 1588

cardinal: a very important priest in the Roman Catholic Church

cargo: goods carried by ship

chancellor: someone who is responsible for a country's money and taxes

constipation: a health problem which makes it difficult to pass faeces (poo)

court: a group of people who are close to a king or queen, and who act as the monarch's advisors and friends

gamekeeper: someone who looks after the birds and animals in a hunting park and who sometimes shoots them if they are needed for food

guardian: an adult who looks after a boy or girl if the child's parents have died

infection: disease in part of the body

inherit: to take over something from another person after he or she has died

ladies-in-waiting: women who act as companions to a princess or a queen

laundry: washing and drying clothes

mercury: a soft metal, which is poisonous

mineral: a kind of rock

minister: a person with an important job in government

monarch: a king or queen

Protestant: belonging to the Christian Church, but not following the Pope in Rome

Roman Catholic Church: belonging to the Christian Church, and following the Pope in Rome

scholar: someone who studies hard and knows lots of things

tutor: a teacher who gives pupils private lessons

FURTHER INFORMATION

MORE BOOKS TO READ

Simon Adams
Tudor (Eyewitness Guide)
(Dorling Kindersley, 2004)

Nicola Barber
Tudor Life: Entertainment and Homes
(Wayland, 2009)

Terry Deary
Terrible Tudors
(Scholastic, 2009)

Katie Dicker
History Detective: A Tudor Theatre (Wayland, 2009)

Liz Gogerly
Tudor Life: Clothes
(Wayland, 2009)

Paul Harrison
Tudor Life: Work
(Wayland, 2009)

Angela Royston
History from Objects: the Tudors
(Wayland, 2010)

Richard Tames
History Detective: Tudor Medicine (Wayland, 2009)

Dereen Taylor
History Detective: A Tudor Home (Wayland, 2009)

USEFUL WEBSITES

www.historyonthenet.com/Tudors/tudorsmain.htm
A very large site on the Tudor period. It includes sections on food, costume and entertainments, and has puzzles and activities.

www.tudorhistory.org
Provides pictures and information on many aspects of Tudor life and history. The site contains links to films featuring the Tudors and sound files of Tudor music.

www.tudorbritain.org
A fun site about Tudor life, created by the Victorian and Albert Museum. Each section has games and quizzes to text your knowledge.

PLACES TO VISIT

Hampton Court Palace, Surrey
http://www.hrp.org.uk/hamptoncourtpalace/
One of Henry VIII's royal palaces. You can visit the largest kitchens in Tudor England, built to feed the 1,200 members of Henry VIII's court twice every day!

Tower of London, London
http://www.hrp.org.uk/TowerOfLondon/
A famous prison in Tudor times. Find out about the Tower's famous prisoners, why they were locked up and what happened to them.

Mary Rose Museum, Portsmouth
http://www.maryrose.org/
An exhibition based around a rescued Tudor ship that sank in 1545, including artefacts recovered from the wreck.

Index

Numbers in **bold** indicate pictures.

advisors 10, 11, **11**
America 21
apothecaries 14, 19
archbishops 10
arithmetic 17

babies 9, 12, 13
beggars 18, **22**

cardinals 10, 11
chancellor 11
Church 6, 10, 11, 15, 26, 27
Cleves, Anne of 11
clothes 6, 13, 13, 14, 20, 22, 22, 23, 23
countryside 12, 15, 17, 18
court 10, 22
craftworkers 20
Cromwell, Thomas 11, **11**

diseases 7, 13, 14, 19
doctors 14, 18, 19
Drake, Sir Francis 6, 21, **21**

education 6, 16, 17
execution 11, 26, 27

families 8, **8**, 12, 14, 15, **15**, 20, 24

farming 18, **18**
food 6, 12, 14, 15, 20

gamekeepers 14
games 13
gardens 12
guardians 7

Hardwick, Bess of 9, **9**, 13
houses 6, 12, **12**, 14
housework 8, 14

landowners 18
Latin 17, 18, 27
laws 10, 22, 23
lawyers 16, 17, 18

market stalls 20, **20**
marriage 9, 11
medicines 19
merchants 11, 16, 20
monarchs 6, 7, **7**, 10, **10**, 11, 13, 16, 17, 19, **23**
 Edward VI 6, 7, **7**, 16, 19
 Elizabeth I 6, 7, **7**, 13, 16, 23, **23**, 25, 27
 Henry VII 6, 7, 11
 Henry VIII 6, 7, **7**, 11, 17, 19, 24, 26
 James I 6
 Mary I 6, 7, **7**, **14**, 27, **27**
Moore, Thomas 11
music 25

pirates 20, 21
poor people 6, 8, 12, 13, 14, **14**, 15, 18, 22, 24

religion 26, 27
rhetoric 17
rich people 6, 8, 9, 12, 13, **13**, 14, 16, 22, **22**, 24, 25

sailors 6, 21
schools 16, **16**, 17
sea captains 20, 21
servants 8, 14
Seymour, Jane 7
Shakespeare, William 6, 25
shops 18, 20, **20**
Skelton, John 17, **17**
soldiers 11, 21
Spanish Armada 6, 21
Stuart, Lady Arbella 13, **13**

theatre 25, **25**
thieves 18
towns 6, 18
toys 13
trade 6
tuberculosis 7
tutors 7, 16

Wolsey, Thomas 11
work 9, 18, **18**, 19, **19**, 20, **20**, 21
worship 10